Celebrate
the Century

A COLLECTION OF
COMMEMORATIVE STAMPS

1910-1919

UNITED STATES POSTAL SERVICE

POSTMASTER GENERAL
AND CHIEF EXECUTIVE OFFICER
Marvin Runyon

CHIEF MARKETING OFFICER AND
SENIOR VICE PRESIDENT
Allen Kane

EXECUTIVE DIRECTOR, STAMP SERVICES
Azeezaly S. Jaffer

MANAGER, STAMP MARKETING
Valoree Vargo

PROJECT MANAGER
Gary A. Thuro Jr.

TIME-LIFE BOOKS IS A DIVISION OF TIME LIFE INC.

TIME-LIFE CUSTOM PUBLISHING

VICE PRESIDENT AND PUBLISHER
Terry Newell

VICE PRESIDENT OF
NEW BUSINESS DEVELOPMENT
Michael A. Hurley

DIRECTOR OF EDITORIAL DEVELOPMENT
Jennifer Louise Pearce

CUSTOM MARKETING MANAGER
John Charles Loyack

EDITORIAL STAFF FOR CELEBRATE THE CENTURY

MANAGING EDITOR
Morin Bishop

EDITORS
Sally Guard, John Bolster

DESIGNER
Barbara Chilenskas

WRITERS
Merrell Noden, Eve Peterson

RESEARCHERS
*Jenny Douglas,
Jessica Goldstein, Lauren Cardonsky*

PHOTO EDITOR
Bill Broyles

LIBRARY OF CONGRESS CATALOGING-IN-PUBLICATION DATA
Celebrate the century: a collection of commemorative stamps.
p. cm. Includes index.
Contents: v. 2. 1910–1919.
ISBN 0-7835-5318-8 (v. 2)
1. Commemorative postage stamps—United States—History—20th century.
2. United States—History—20th century.
I. Time-Life Books
HE6185.U5C45 1998   97–46952
769.56973—DC21   CIP

Books produced by Time-Life Custom Publishing are available at a special bulk discount for promotional and premium use. Custom adaptations can also be created to meet your specific marketing goals. Call 1-800-323-5255.

PICTURE CREDITS

Cover, Hulton Getty/Tony Stone Images; 4, Corbis-Bettmann; 5, Culver Pictures; 6, Brown Brothers; 7, Brown Brothers; 8, Culver Pictures; 9, Corbis-Bettmann; 10, Philadelphia Museum of Art, The Louise and Walter Arensberg Collection; 11, top, Archives of American Art, Smithsonian Institution, inset (stamp), *Nude Descending a Staircase* ©Duchamp/ARS; 12, top, Archives of American Art, Smithsonian Institution; bottom, Brown Brothers; 13, Metropolitan Museum of Art, The Alfred Stieglitz Collection; 14, top, Archives of American Art, Smithsonian Institution; inset, Lee Stalsworth/Hirshhorn Museum and Sculpture Garden, Smithsonian Institution, Gift of Joseph H. Hirshorn, 1966; 15, Thannhauser Collection, The Solomon R. Guggenheim Museum, New York, David Heald ©The Solomon R. Guggenheim Foundation, New York; 16, Archive Photos; 17, Archive Photos/Popperfoto; 18, left, Archive Photos/American Stock; 18-19, Brown Brothers; 19, right, Hulton Getty/Tony Stone Images; 20, Corbis-Bettmann; 21, left, UPI/Corbis-Bettman, right, Archive Photos/American Stock; 22, Corbis-Bettman; 23, Corbis-Bettman; 24, Corbis-Bettman; 25, top, UPI/Corbis-Bettmann, bottom, Tuskegee University Archives; 26, Tuskegee University Archives; 27, top, Corbis-Bettmann, bottom, UPI/Corbis-Bettmann; 28, Archive Photos; 29, top Brown Brothers, inset (stamp), Charlie Chaplin™ ©Bubbles Inc., S.A.; 30, top, Archive Photos, bottom, Brown Brothers; 31, top, Archive Photos, bottom left, Archive Photos, bottom right, Brown Brothers; 32, Kino International; 33, top, Brown Brothers, bottom, Archive Photos/Popperfoto; 34, New York Public Library; 35, Brown Brothers; 36, top, New York Public Library, bottom, New York Public Library; 37, top, Brown Brothers, bottom, New York Public Library; 38, left, New York Public Library, right, Brown Brothers; 39, top, Brown Brothers, bottom, Brown Brothers; 40, Culver Pictures; 41, Culver Pictures; 42, left, Hulton Getty/Tony Stone Images; 42-43, Brown Brothers; 43, top, Brown Brothers, bottom, Brown Brothers; 44, inset, Culver Pictures; 44-45, Culver Pictures; 45, top, Culver Pictures, bottom, Hulton Getty/Tony Stone Images; 46, The Will Shortz Collection; 47; The Will Shortz Collection; 48, The Will Shortz Collection; 49, top left, AP/World Wide Photos, top right, The Will Shortz Collection, middle right, The Will Shortz Collection; 50, UPI/Corbis-Bettmann; 51, top, UPI/Corbis-Bettmann, inset (stamp), Jack Dempsey™ Estate of Jack Dempsey c/o CMG Worldwide, Indpl, IN.; 52-53, Archive Photos/Hirz; 53, top right, UPI/Corbis-Bettmann, bottom, Archive Photos/Hirz; 54, inset, Archive Photos; 54-55, Archive Photos/Hirz; 55, Archive Photos; 56, Underwood Photo Archives; 57, Joel Perlin Collection; 58, New York Public Library; 59, top, Joel Perlin Collection, bottom left, Joseph W. Lauher Collection, bottom right, Joel Perlin Collection; 60, top, Joel Perlin Collection, bottom, Arlan Coffman Collection; 61, all, Arlan Coffman Collection; 62, Brown Brothers; 63, Brown Brothers; 64, The U.S. Senate Collection, Center for Legislative Archives; 65, Brown Brothers; 66, Brown Brothers; 67, Brown Brothers; 68, top left, Culver Pictures, middle left, Brown Brothers; 68-69, Underwood Photo Archives, SF; 69, right, Underwood Photo Archives, SF; 70, Underwood Photo Archives, SF; 71, top, Brown Brothers, bottom, Culver Pictures; 72, Archive Photos; 73, Hulton Getty/Tony Stone Images; 74, top, Archive Photos, bottom, Archive Photos; 75, left, Underwood & Underwood/Corbis-Bettmann, right, Mary Evans Picture Library; 76, Underwood Photo Archives, SF; 77, top left, Brown Brothers, top right, Brown Brothers, inset, Archive Photos; 78, Brown Brothers; 79, Brown Brothers; 80, top left, Archive Photos, bottom left, Archive Photos; 80-81, Brown Brothers; 81, top, Brown Brothers, bottom, Brown Brothers; 82, top, Brown Brothers, bottom, Brown Brothers; 83, top, Culver Pictures, bottom, Mary Evans Picture Library; 84, Brown Brothers; 85, Brown Brothers; 86, top, Corbis-Bettmann, bottom, Underwood Photo Archives, SF; 87, top, Archive Photos, bottom, Archive Photos; 88, left, Brown Brothers, right, Archive Photos; 89, top, Brown Brothers, bottom, Underwood Photo Archives, SF; 90, Culver Pictures; 91, top, UPI/Corbis-Bettmann inset (stamp), Jim Thorpe™ Family of Jim Thorpe c/o CMG Worldwide, Indpl, IN.; 92, top, Culver Pictures, bottom, Popperfoto; 93, Culver Pictures; 94, top, Culver Pictures, bottom, Archive Photos; 95, top, Corbis-Bettmann, bottom, Culver Pictures.

CONTENTS

Wilson (with second wife, Edith, right) was responsible for committing U.S. troops (above) to the Allied cause.

INTRODUCTION

Things fall apart; the centre cannot hold;
Mere anarchy is loosed upon the world,
The blood-dimmed tide is loosed, and everywhere
The ceremony of innocence is drowned.

William Butler Yeats was Irish, of course, not American. But in *The Second Coming*, which was published in 1920, he captured perfectly the sense of confusion, chaos and anxiety that had swept through the entire Western world in the previous 10 years.

World War I—the Great War—was partly to blame. In many European countries it had wiped out an entire generation. More chillingly, it was the first "modern" war, meaning that the recent boom in technology made killing a less personal task and a far more efficient one. Suddenly, one of the nineteenth century's greatest articles of faith stood refuted: Science, technology and machinery

didn't necessarily lead to progress. They brought death, which now came in many ingenious forms: It could fall from the sky as bombs, strike from submarines under the sea, or steal silently across the fields in clouds of poison gas.

The United States entered the war relatively late, in April of 1917, and its casualties, while great, were nothing compared to those suffered in Europe. But one didn't have to go to war to feel as if treasured, familiar institutions were under attack right here in the United States.

Everywhere one looked, one saw threats to the comfortable old order: radical unions such as the Wobblies; subversive European art like Marcel Duchamp's *Nude Descending a Staircase*; women not only demanding the right to vote but also smoking openly.

And one could no longer just turn one's back on it all, since the country was more crowded than

ever. During this decade, the U.S. population jumped past the 100-million mark for the first time, reaching 106,021,537 in the census of 1920. Of these new Americans, almost a million a year were immigrants. And according to the Bureau of the Census, in 1920, for the first time, more people lived in cities than in rural areas. By the time Robert Frost, the laureate of the New England woods, published his first volume of poetry, *A Boy's Will*, in 1913, it seemed as if the forests were shrinking before the relentlessly expanding cities. In contrast to Frost's meditations on nature was the work of Carl Sandburg, who celebrated chaotic cities like Chicago as hives of work and life: "Hog Butcher for the World/Tool Maker, Stacker of Wheat,/Player with Railroads and the Nation's Freight Handler;/Stormy, husky, brawling,/City of the Big Shoulders."

It was a time of tremendous upheaval and dislocation. Propelled by Henry Ford's popular Model T, four million of which were on the roads by the end of the decade, and by the telephone, which linked the coasts in 1915, the pace of life was accelerating at a frightening rate, forcing people to reinvent their lives. Large segments of the population were demanding new rights and new roles. The Great Migration of black Americans from the rural South to the urban North began in earnest around 1915, the same year that women marched up Fifth Avenue demanding the right to vote. In times like these,

Millions of Americans were infatuated with Chaplin's antics.

it was easy to be nostalgic for the Good Old Days just one generation earlier, when people knew their places, knew their neighbors, and knew what shape their lives would assume.

In many ways, these disturbing times seemed to beg for a leader like Theodore Roosevelt, a man who was the embodiment of decisiveness. Roosevelt did run for president in 1912—for what would have been an unprecedented third term, on the Progressive "Bull Moose" ticket. But he succeeded only in siphoning votes from William Howard Taft, the Republican, thereby ensuring the triumph of a man who could not have been more unlike him in temperament, Woodrow Wilson. "I am a vague, conjectural personality," Wilson once wrote of himself, "more made up of opinions and academic prepossessions than of human traits and red corpuscles."

Wilson had very little experience in practical politics. Having distinguished himself first as a historian and then as president of Princeton University, he had been elected governor of New Jersey in 1910, and surprised everyone by turning out to be not only an activist but a successful one too. As president, Wilson was to dominate the second decade of the century much the way Roosevelt had the first. Indeed, the election of 1912 marked a major shift in American politics, with Wilson's Democrats becoming the party with new ideas.

As remote and intellectual as he was, Wilson understood the unsavory way big money and big business were undermining democracy. "It is of serious interest to the country," he said, "that the people at large should have no lobby while great bodies of astute men seek to create an artificial opinion and to overcome the interests of the public for their private profit."

Calling for government to be "put at the service of humanity," Wilson pushed through a wide variety of progressive, protective legislation. One of his first orders of business was to shepherd and then sign into law the Federal Reserve Act, which reorganized and strengthened the U.S. banking and currency system, ensuring that nothing like the financial panic of 1907 would occur again. The following year Congress wrote two of Wilson's favorite schemes into law, establishing the Federal Trade Commission and passing the Clayton Antitrust Act, which attacked monopolies while buttressing workers' right to strike.

It is a measure of both Wilson's courage and the progressive temper of the times that he was able to accomplish so much. With war already under way in Europe and the Russian Revolution soon to replace the Tsars with the Bolsheviks, the specter of unruly masses appeared on this side of the Atlantic. In 1914 a seven-month strike by 9,000 Colorado coal miners was broken up by vigilantes who attacked the workers' encampment, raking it with gunfire and killing at least 21 men. In the first six months of 1916 alone, there were 2,093 strikes or lock-

The scandal of child labor revealed the underside of America's growth.

outs, many of which ended in vicious reprisals.

The most violent reprisals were reserved for the most radical of all unions, the Industrial Workers of the World, or Wobblies, which had been founded in 1905 and at every opportunity justified its reputation for revolutionary rhetoric and violence. In 1912 the I.W.W. took control of a textile workers' strike in Lawrence, Massachusetts, and shocked the middle class with its brashly leftist slogans.

With the national mood one of barely restrained paranoia, it was especially dangerous to be foreign or different. In 1913, a Georgia jury convicted Leo Frank, the manager of an Atlanta pencil factory who happened to be Jewish, of murder on highly suspect evidence. When the governor commuted his death sentence, a mob snatched Frank from his jail cell and lynched him.

Civil liberties were often sacrificed. On January 16, 1919, Congress ratified the Eighteenth Amendment, which prohibited the transport, manufacture or sale of alcoholic beverages; "prohibition" would remain the law of the land for 14 years. Later in 1919, in Schenck v. United States, the U.S. Supreme Court affirmed the Espionage Act of 1917, ruling that first amendment rights to free speech and the press could be abridged if "the words are of such a nature and used in such circumstance as to create a clear and present danger."

As Wilson knew well, the divide between rich

The completion of the Panama Canal was just one of Wilson's many interests in Latin America.

and poor was growing wider. For those who were lucky enough to be on the right side of the divide, life was wonderful.

The Model T bestowed unprecedented freedom of movement, and more and more people were attending sporting events, including professional baseball games, featuring spindly-legged Boston Red Sox slugger Babe Ruth, or one of Jack Dempsey's heavyweight title fights. For more sedate amusement, there were movies, many of them starring either Mary Pickford or Charlie Chaplin, and crossword puzzles, which were invented in 1913.

For the poor, of course, life was a much grimmer business. On March 25, 1911, a fire at the Triangle Shirtwaist Company in New York City killed 146 workers, many of them immigrant women who were trapped on the top three floors of the 10-story Asch Building.

Children too were sacrificed on the altar of greed. Stirred by Lewis Wickes Hine's photographs of some of the two million children under the age of 16 who were working full time in 1911, Wilson used his moral force to push through the Keating-Owen Act of 1916, which banned articles produced by child labor. Unfortu-

nately, the Supreme Court ruled the law unconstitutional just two years later.

Though Wilson seemed to have work enough staying on top of domestic affairs, he was also tremendously active abroad. Latin America was of special interest to him, especially with the opening of the Panama Canal in 1914. In an early speech Wilson had assured Latin American nations that his aim was "to cultivate the friendship and deserve the confidence" of their people. In practice, however, he continued Taft's "dollar diplomacy," signing a treaty with Nicaragua to protect American access to the Panama Canal; sending the Marines into Haiti, where they stayed from 1915 through 1934, and into the Dominican Republic, where they remained for eight years. He did use force in a more idealistic cause in Mexico, however, exercising American might to aid the forces of democracy and produce a Mexican constitution in 1917.

But Wilson's biggest foreign policy question was obviously the war in Europe, which had commenced, to the total shock of most Americans, in 1914. Wilson had hoped to remain neutral, actually campaigning in 1916 with the slogan, "he kept us out of war." But neutrality rapidly became a difficult stance to defend, especially after the Germans sank the British liner *Lusitania*, killing more than 1,000 people including 128 Americans. When in early 1917 Germany announced the reopening of unrestricted submarine warfare and quickly sank eight American ships, Wilson had no choice but to break his promise. On April 2, 1917, he asked Congress for a declaration of war and four days later he got it.

The United States entered the Great War at a critical time, for the Allies were in serious trouble on several fronts. In October, the Italian army had been defeated at Caporetto, while the

A parade in New York celebrated the war's end, but Americans were left with a sense of unease about their world.

Russians, reeling from the revolution at home, were petitioning for peace. Germany, meanwhile, was preparing a knockout blow against weary Britain and France, rushing 40 new divisions into France. In a timely demonstration of American willpower, the United States sent ship after ship of soldiers across the Atlantic, 80,000 in March, 118,000 in April and almost 250,000 in May. They clearly made the difference. "The tide of war," wrote General John Pershing, "was definitely turned in favor of the Allies."

The Great War ended on November 11, 1918. In less than a year of real fighting, more than 106,000 U.S. soldiers had died, at least half of them from pneumonia. In January of 1919, Wilson went to Paris hoping to convince other nations to adopt his idealistic Fourteen Points for peace, which included unrestricted shipping, dis-

armament, the reduction of tariffs, and the thing closest to the idealistic Wilson's heart, a League of Nations to prevent further wars.

A disappointed Wilson came home with a watered-down version of his plan. He won the Nobel Peace Prize for 1919 and set out on a national tour to persuade the American people to embrace the League, suffering a stroke while traveling. His Republican successor, Warren G. Harding, campaigned against the League, arguing that "we seek no part in directing the destinies of the world." Though Wilson's idealistic League of Nations was voted down by Congress in 1920, its aim lives on today in the United Nations. At the urging of the cerebral Wilson, the United States had flexed its muscles for the first time on the world stage. The world took note of this powerful young giant of a nation. It does to this day.

THE ARMORY SHOW

Today, when much of the public dismisses modern art as maddeningly unfathomable or totally irrelevant, it is hard to appreciate the power of the cultural bombshell that dropped on New York City when the International Exhibition of Modern Art opened on February 17, 1913. Everyone talked about it, everyone had an opinion—having seen the show or not. "No exhibition had ever had such a media blitz," writes Robert Hughes in his magisterial *American Visions: The Epic History of Art in America.* "For once, here was an art event that had the crunch of real news, the latest murder or the newest political scandal."

"The Armory Show," as it was known to the hundreds of thousands of Americans who saw it and were either scandalized or inspired by it, was probably the most important art show of this century. It introduced the radical new art of Europe to a country that had been too busy growing and getting rich to pay much attention to the rest of the world. Ironically, in doing so, it started a shift in the center of art power from the Old World, where it had resided unchallenged for centuries, to the New, where it remains to this day. "This man [Arthur B. Davies] has started something," said the painter Leon Dabo. "I'm afraid it may be more of a calamity than a blessing, though it's a damn good show."

Indeed it was, at least for those viewers willing to enter with an open mind. Filling 18 huge rooms with an estimated 1,300 works, the show was enormous, chaotic, overwhelming and mind-bending. Here were irony, irreverence, absurdity and incongruity—all the ingredients of modernism—served up in great quantity. Included was virtually every major artist of the period: Pablo Picasso, Constantin Brancusi, Marcel Duchamp, Francis Picabia, Auguste Rodin, Georges Seurat, Paul Cézanne,

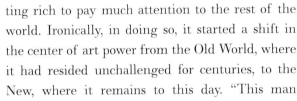

One critic at the Armory Show (top) saw Duchamp's *Nude Descending a Staircase* (left) as "an explosion in a shingle factory."

11

The show's 1,300 works included sculpture (top) as well as paintings by artists such as Duchamp (above) and Kandinsky, whose *Garden of Love (Improvisation # 27)* (opposite page) illustrated the shift away from representation and toward abstraction.

Georges Braque and Paul Gaugin. There were 18 Van Goghs and 17 Matisses. In hindsight, the prices look silly: Matisse's *Red Studio* went unsold at $4,050, Cézanne's *Bathers* at $6,500. The Armory Show was the brainchild of Davies, a symbolist painter and somewhat unlikely revolutionary, since his own work tended toward the coolly classical, featuring unicorns and nymphs. In the summer of 1912, Davies saw a catalog of the Sonderbund exhibit in Cologne, which included many works by Van Gogh, Cézanne, Gaugin and Picasso, among many, many others. Bowled over by it, he wired his friend Walt Kuhn in New York, saying, "I wish we could have a show like this." Almost immediately Kuhn sailed for Europe, arriving on the last day of the Sonderbund show, which stunned and inspired him. He began traveling through Europe, persuading collectors and artists to contribute to the Armory Show. Overwhelmed by the task, he summoned Davies and the two

"This exhibition will be epoch making in the history of American art. Tonight will be the red-letter night in the history not only of American but of all modern art."

—*JOHN QUINN, legal adviser to the organizers, in his comments opening the show, 1913*

The poster for the show (left) helped to draw up to 10,000 visitors per day into the armory's cleverly divided space (above) where they viewed a stunning collection of works that included Van Gogh's *Mountains at Saint-Rémy* (opposite page).

friends spent weeks convincing the continent's greatest artists to support their effort.

They had considered holding the exhibit in Madison Square Garden, but when that proved too expensive they settled for the cavernous, turreted 69th Regiment Armory, on Lexington Avenue between 25th and 26th Streets. They could have used more space: Day after day, Lexington Avenue was bumper-to-bumper with hansoms. Some days as many as 10,000 people made their way through the exhibit. Half the fun lay in "interpreting" the outlandish works. One wag described Brancusi's

Mlle. Pogany as "a hardboiled egg balanced on a cube of sugar." Picasso too was a favorite target.

Still, most critics saved their deadliest venom for Duchamp's *Nude Descending a Staircase*, that now familiar, muted brown, bell-bottomed figure that seems to have been shot in stop-motion photography while walking down stairs. Nudes—at least those in the art world—had never been depicted doing anything other than reclining or standing motionless. Duchamp's painting was a special favorite of those who came to the show determined to be outraged. To them, it resembled "a lot of

disused golf clubs," a "dynamited suit of Japanese armor," or "an explosion in a shingle factory." The irreverent Frenchman was almost as delighted by the uproar as he was by the fact that the painting sold for $324.

From New York, the show traveled to Chicago—where art students burned Matisse and Brancusi in effigy—and then to Boston. By the time the pieces were packed away, some 300,000 people had paid the price of admission, few of whom could have known that they were paying for a glimpse of the future.

Aftermath

The new modes of seeing and depicting the world—indeed the move in some instances to pure abstraction—continued to dominate the art world for decades to come, with giants such as Robert Rauschenberg, Willem de Kooning and others picking up where Picasso, Kandinsky and Matisse left off. To this day, so-called modern or postmodern art provokes strong reactions—admiration in some, scorn in others, but rarely indifference.

WORLD WAR I

Most people remember that World War I was triggered by the assassination of Austria-Hungary's Archduke Ferdinand and his wife, Sophie, in 1914. Perhaps fewer know that the assassin who fired the Great War's first shot was a mere schoolboy. Gavrilo Princip, a Bosnian grammar school student, stepped onto the running board of the Archduke's car, which had momentarily stopped on a street in Sarajevo, and killed Ferdinand with one shot and Sophie with another, setting in motion a chain of events that would lead to the deaths of at least eight

million people in a war so bloody and dark and futile it would cause humanity to question its most fundamental assumptions about itself.

The twentieth century to that point had been about progress, the widely held notion that humanity was engaged in a gradual process of betterment. World War I, with its savage trench war-

fare, poison gas, machine guns and long-range artillery, brought about death on a scale never before imagined, and the horror left much of the world stripped of its idealism. Every nation involved mobilized forces of unprecedented mass only to quickly lose control of them. What many had thought would be a swift and decisive conflict rapidly descended into a nightmare of attrition. The photographs of World War I battlefields are pictures of desolation: bombed-out moonscapes stretch to the horizon littered with dead horses and strewn with barbed wire and splintered tree stumps. Writer Philip Gibbs interviewed a German prisoner captured in France during the war:

"How will it end?" I asked.

"I see no end to it," he answered. "It is the suicide of nations...."

The war did finally end, in 1918, largely due to

Marches (top, in New York) produced huge numbers of U.S. recruits, who aided the Allies in France (left) and elsewhere.

17

"I can see no excuse for deceiving you about these four days. I have suffered seventh hell. I have not been at the front. I have been in front of it."
—*WILFRED OWEN, poet, writing to his mother, 1917*

Newspaper reports of the sinking of the *Lusitania* (left) helped to persuade the public that war was necessary; watched by awe-struck children, U.S. troops swept through France (above), enabling the Allies to bring an end to the years of brutal trench warfare (opposite page, right).

Germany torpedoed the British liner *Lusitania*, killing more than 1,000 people, 128 of them Americans. Wilson issued a stern warning, ordering Germany to abandon its U-boat attacks in the waters surrounding the British Isles, but still refused to enter the war. When Germany declared all-out war at sea in 1917 and began attacking indiscriminately, more American ships and citizens perished. His tolerance at an end, Wilson asked Congress to declare war in April, and the United States joined the fray that summer, providing the exhausted and depleted Allies with support they desperately needed.

Mobilizing the American force was a complex and weighty task. The United States had not mounted a major war effort in 50 years and was woefully unprepared and underequipped. The U.S. Army consisted of a paltry 208,034 men. One of Wilson's first acts after Congress declared war was the establishment of the Committee on Public Information (CPI), an organization headed by crusading magazine writer George Creel. Also known as the Creel Committee, CPI was a collection of

the mobilization of American forces, which tipped the balance in favor of the Allies. President Woodrow Wilson had maintained a firm policy of neutrality during the first three years of the war, even as German attacks at sea put U.S. merchants and travelers at risk. On May 7, 1915,

journalists, psychologists, artists, film directors and scholars whose task it was to generate propaganda to rally domestic support for the war effort. They saturated the nation with fact books about the Allies and the enemy, distributed abridged versions of Wilson's speeches on the war and papered the country with posters, the most famous of which was James Montgomery Flagg's "I Want You" painting. Actually a self-portrait, the poster depicts a stern-looking Flagg in an Uncle Sam costume complete with star-spangled top hat, pointing a finger straight at his audience as the admonition roars above him.

Millions of these were issued and, indeed, Uncle Sam got what he wanted. The Selective Service Act, which Wilson pressured Congress to approve in May, swelled the size of Uncle Sam's army to four million by the end of the war. A colossal domestic effort also went forward. Factories ran 24 hours a day. Grocers di-

verted tons of food to the U.S. "doughboys," and women filled the jobs the draftees left behind.

By 1918 two million Americans had served in Europe under General John Pershing's command. They forged a successful assault on the German war machine, culminating in the 47-day offensive launched at Meuse-Argonne on Sept. 26, 1918. Despite logistical and command difficulties, the Americans prevailed, crippling the German forces by late October and bringing the bloody war to an end on Nov. 11.

Aftermath

One could certainly argue that World War I was the beginning of the modern era. The suspicion of idealism, the sense that technology can be turned against its creators in brutal ways, the notion that so-called progress often carries an awesome price are all contemporary concepts traceable to that bloody and senseless conflict. The disillusionment that stemmed from those insights would forever change the nature of art, literature, music, and indeed, the very way in which humanity viewed itself. The human tragedies to follow simply made these points ever more inescapable.

GEORGE WASHINGTON CARVER

George Washington Carver was not your typical hard-nosed scientist. Here was a man who loved to paint and draw, referred to his laboratory as "God's little workshop," and rejected formal garb in favor of tattered shoes and rumpled jackets with a fresh flower unfailingly placed in his lapel.

Along the way, the so-called "Wizard of Tuskegee" revolutionized agricultural practices in the South by championing a system of crop rotation in the second decade of the century, became an authority on plant disease and discovered some 300 uses for the peanut, thereby emerging as the leading symbol of black achievement in the period between World War I and World War II.

Carver's path to celebrity was not an easy one. Born a slave in Diamond Grove, Missouri, around 1861—the records for slaves were not always carefully maintained—Carver and his mother were kidnapped shortly thereafter by nightriders with plans to sell them farther south. The baby was soon returned by vigilantes (in exchange for a $300 racehorse), but Carver's mother was not to be heard from again. Though his former owners, Moses and Susan Carver, assumed the task of raising him to adulthood and by all reports treated him as their own son, a sense of loneliness forged from this formative experience would accompany Carver throughout his life.

Carver struggled for 20 years to receive a formal education. At 12, he was barred from attending a local church on the grounds of his race, and he was later denied admission at Highland College for the same reason. By the time he finally enrolled as a freshman at Simpson College in Indianola, Iowa, he was 30.

In 1896, having transferred to Iowa State Agriculture College—now Iowa State—and received a bachelors and a masters degree, Carver was asked by Booker T. Washington to become head of the agriculture department at The Tuskegee Institute

Whether in his laboratory (left) or his greenhouse (top), Carver was a tireless worker throughout his life.

"Carver saved the South. He is to the peanut what Edison was to the lightbulb."

—FRANK GODDEN, historian for the Tuskegee Alumni Association, 1996

in Alabama, then a struggling black trade school. Carver would remain at Tuskegee for the rest of his life, and it was there that he developed the groundbreaking ideas for which he is famous.

In response to complaints by southern farmers, who were faced with nutrient-poor soil as a result of their decision to plant nothing but cotton season after season, Carver proposed a crop-rotation method, which alternated nitrate-producing legumes, such as peanuts and peas, with cotton. The result was newly revitalized soil, thankful farmers—and a bounty of new crops.

Among Carver's multiple uses for the newly plentiful peanut were antiseptic soap, fuel briquettes, laxatives, cooking oil, printer's ink, shaving cream and paper, but apparently not peanut butter, though he is credited with popularizing the product. After he found that the sweet potato and the pecan also enriched depleted soils, he went on to find scores of uses for them, too.

Throughout his life he remained deeply religious. The boy who had "literally lived in the woods, wanting to know every strange stone, flower and insect" now rose at 4 a.m. for a daily walk amidst his beloved flowers and plants. "I love to think of nature as an unlimited broadcasting system through which God speaks to us every hour, if we only tune in," he explained.

Carver's deep concern for the state of the southern soil (opposite page) led him to develop a system of crop rotation based on his beloved peanut (left), just one of the many accomplishments that drew admiring visitors such as Franklin Roosevelt (above).

In 1921, Carver spoke before a House committee on the issue of a tariff for peanuts. Members laughed as he pulled out samples of the many products he had based on the peanut. "Do you want a watermelon to go along with that?" asked one narrowminded congressman. Yet even in the face of such obvious prejudice Carver was never an outspoken critic of bigotry, opting instead to bow to "Jim Crow"—the laws that enforced segregation—and cultivate the friendship of influential whites who might serve as patrons for him and other aspiring blacks. That strategy paid off in Carver's long battle to be schooled, and would pay off to a large degree in adulthood: Among Carver's many white friends in later life was Henry Ford, who eventually offered him hundreds of thousands of dollars to leave Tuskegee and become a plastics engineer. Carver refused, preferring to remain at his beloved Tuskegee.

At the time of his death in 1943, Carver was probably the best-known and most respected black figure in America, esteemed by blacks and whites in much the same way as Booker T. Washington had been earlier and Martin Luther King Jr. would be later.

Aftermath

Time has tempered Carver's legacy somewhat. "The very qualities that made him a hero to Americans in the 1940s and 1950s made him suspect among blacks and liberals in the 1960s," observes Gary R. Kremer in his 1987 book *George Washington Carver in His Own Words.* Older, stooped, celibate and humble, Carver, a once-perfect symbol for black achievement, became a good deal less so in the face of the civil rights movement and Malcolm X and other more radical black voices. But hindsight is always a poor—and often unfair—means of judging character; Carver's accomplishment in moving from slave to student to scientist remains worthy of admiration.

Carver spent the last 47 years of his life at Tuskegee, where he taught groups of students (left) and individuals (above) alike; even in 1940, just three years before his death, Carver (right) kept working in his lab and remained fascinated by the world of nature.

CHARLIE CHAPLIN

Of all the great icons the movies have given us— John Wayne and Marilyn Monroe, James Dean and Humphrey Bogart—none has lingered as long in our hearts or wielded as much emotional power as Charlie Chaplin's little tramp. Chaplin formally introduced the now familiar, wobbly little figure with its baggy pants, bowler hat, brush moustache and cane in 1915, in *The Tramp*, but he had been working on it in one form or another for years, since his days as an English music hall performer. Because he did not speak, Chaplin's tramp was a deep mine of emotion. Above all, he stood for human dignity and hope in a world that was hostile to those things.

The Tramp marked the beginning of what *Motion Picture Magazine* called "Chaplinitis," a delirium every bit as powerful as Beatlemania. Almost overnight Chaplin became the biggest star of the silent film era. Tin Pan Alley turned out songs honoring him, from "The Chaplin Waddle" to "The Charlie Strut," and Charlie Chaplin dolls, ties, hats and playing cards soon appeared. Other actors rushed to imitate him, including one who called himself Charles Alpin. By 1920, Chaplin had become, according to his friend Max Eastman, "the most famous man in the world, not excepting President Wilson."

He was also an extraordinarily wealthy man, who signed Hollywood's first million-dollar contract, in 1917, and two years later teamed up with Mary Pickford, Douglas Fairbanks and D.W. Griffith to form United Artists. He surely earned both the money and the acclaim. This one-man filmmaking team, who frequently wrote, acted, directed and produced his films, even composed the scores for many of them. One of his classics, *Limelight*, won an Academy Award upon its re-release in 1972. "At his best, he was the greatest comedian who

Chaplin, the antic performer (top), also incorporated a dose of pathos into films such as *The Kid* (left, with Jackie Coogan).

ever lived," said Buster Keaton, who would know.

Trying to understand Chaplin's art by scrutinizing his past is a tricky business, for Chaplin's memory was not to be trusted. Either from shame, or perhaps from a heartwrenching desire to reach back in time and change the painful circumstances of his past, Chaplin was evasive about the details of his boyhood in London, sugarcoating it in places and exaggerating its grimness elsewhere.

In the autobiography he wrote when he was 75, Chaplin claimed he was born in London on April 16, 1889. His parents were both music hall performers, and that hectic, itinerant life took a terrible toll on the young couple, who split up when Charlie was one. Though Charles Chaplin Sr. would drink himself to death at an early age, it was Hannah whose suffering haunted her second son. Tormented by what today we would probably call schizophrenia, she was in and out of mental

Chaplin films include *The Gold Rush* (bottom, 1925), *Shoulder Arms* (opposite page, top, a short from 1918) and *Modern Times* (opposite page, 1936); along with his numerous films came the posters that promoted them (below and right).

"From New York to San Francisco, from Maine to California, came the staccato tapping of the telegraph key. 'Who is this man Chaplin?' The newspapers wanted to know; the country had risen and demanded information."

—*MOTION PICTURE MAGAZINE, 1915*

hospitals for much of her adult life. "Sometimes at night she came into my bed and cried herself to sleep with her arms around me," Chaplin recalled, "and I was so miserable that I wanted to scream."

Like Charles Dickens, Chaplin turned the terror and uncertainty of his childhood into art, becoming the protector and poet of traumatized children. "On the screen," said his friend Thomas Burke, "he is still the wounded boy of fourteen, trying to hide his hurt by self-consolatory antics; and every film of his, from the early crude things down to the more sensitive and considered productions asks help for the young and the wounded."

Chaplin came to the United States in 1913 as part of a touring company of English actors. He was spotted by Adam Kessel, who signed him to Keystone films. Chaplin made an astonishing 35 films for Keystone in 1914, and soon was directing himself. Behind the camera, Chaplin quickly distanced himself from Mack Sennett's frenetic pace and violent slapstick. For Chaplin, comedy had to come from character, not from external events.

Chaplin's empathy for the suffering underdog was instinctual and deep, and it was evident not just on the screen, but also in his life and politics, which were decidedly leftist. They got him into trouble in 1952. After traveling to London for the premier of *Limelight,* Chaplin found that his re-entry permit to the United States had been revoked by James McGranery, the attorney general, who was deeply offended by what he described as Chaplin's "leering, sneering attitude" toward his adopted land. Chaplin refused to submit to INS interrogation, and settled instead in Switzerland, where he and his third wife, Oona O'Neill, raised a large family.

Eventually forgiven his politics, Chaplin returned to the United States in 1972 to receive a second honorary Oscar to join the one he had been given in 1928. When Chaplin died on Christmas morning, 1977, the world lost one of its most original artists.

Chaplin was a wealthy man—before turning 30 he had signed Hollywood's first millon-dollar contract (in 1917) and two years later he joined Mary Pickford and Douglas Fairbanks (opposite page) to form United Artists with D.W. Griffith.

Aftermath

Chaplin's heirs have become legion as comedians have continued to explore the freedom of silent comedy. First, of course, there was Buster Keaton, just six years younger than Chaplin and his costar in *Limelight*. After Keaton came Harpo Marx and the French mime Marcel Marceau. Most recently, Rowan Atkinson's hapless Mr. Bean has continued the tradition of pulling laughs from silence.

CHILD LABOR

The lucky ones swept the trash and filth from city streets, or stood for hours on street corners hawking newspapers. The less fortunate coughed constantly through 10-hour shifts in dark, damp coal mines or sweated to the point of dehydration while tending fiery glass-factory furnaces—all to stoke the profit margins of industrialists whose own childen sat comfortably at school desks gleaning moral principles from their McGuffey *Readers.*

By and large, these child laborers were the sons and daughters of poor parents or recent immigrants who depended on their children's meager wages to survive. But they were also the offspring of the rapid, unchecked industrialization that characterized large American cities as early as the

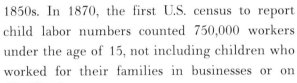

1850s. In 1870, the first U.S. census to report child labor numbers counted 750,000 workers under the age of 15, not including children who worked for their families in businesses or on farms. By 1911, more than two million American children under the age of 16 were working—many of them 12 hours or more, six days a week. Often they toiled in unhealthful and hazardous conditions; always for minuscule wages.

But until the documentary photographs of Lewis Wickes Hine appeared in popular and progressive publications in the teens, the public turned a blind eye to the pervasive and cruel exploitation of children in the workplace. Hine had been hired by the National Child Labor Committee (NCLC)—a

While girls faced the dangers of the spinning bobbins (left), boys (top) descended to dangerous jobs in the mines.

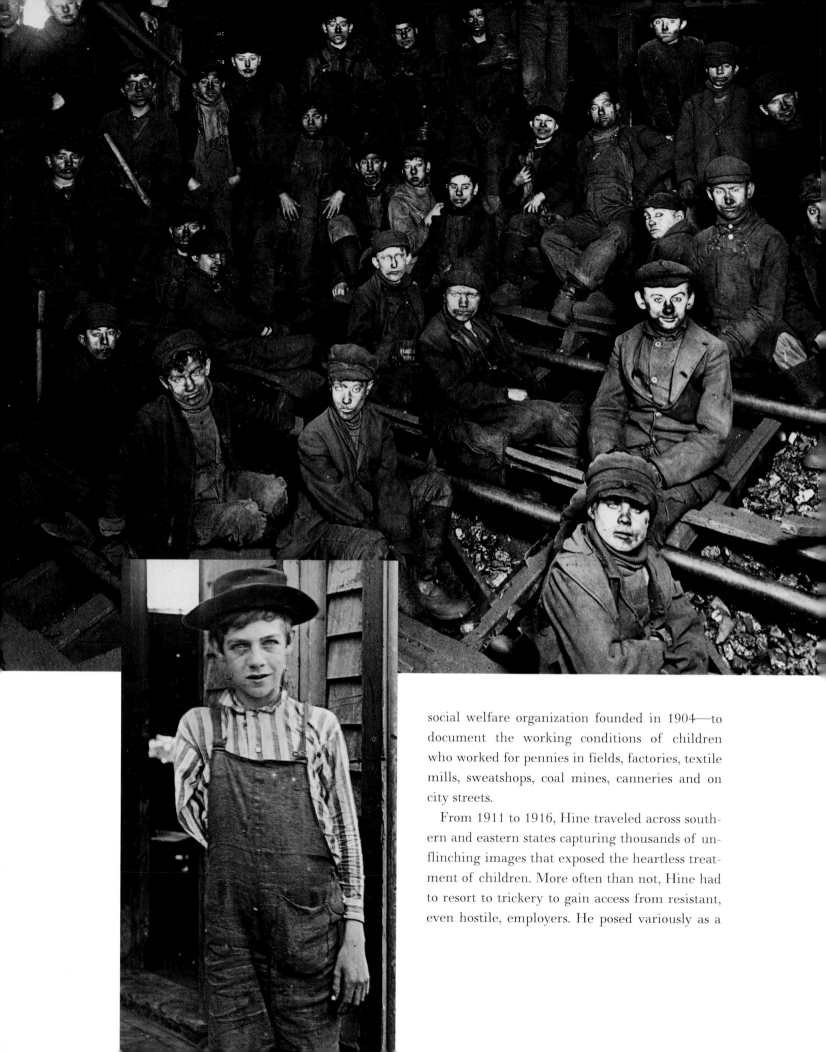

social welfare organization founded in 1904—to document the working conditions of children who worked for pennies in fields, factories, textile mills, sweatshops, coal mines, canneries and on city streets.

From 1911 to 1916, Hine traveled across southern and eastern states capturing thousands of unflinching images that exposed the heartless treatment of children. More often than not, Hine had to resort to trickery to gain access from resistant, even hostile, employers. He posed variously as a

"I wanted to show things that had to be corrected."
—LEWIS WICKES HINE, *social photographer*

Bible salesman, industrial photographer, fire inspector and insurance agent to get candid shots, sometimes with a hidden camera. Children might be removed from view before he arrived or he might be barred from the premises altogether. When Hine couldn't find a way in, he waited outside the gates and photographed the children as they entered and exited.

Hine's pictures were critical evidence in disproving those who denied the existence of exploitive conditions. As such they became the NCLC's most powerful weapons, enabling the Committee to garner broad public support for the cause by exposing wretched working conditions and their harmful effects on innocent children, some as young as six.

The NCLC was not alone in decrying child labor. Numerous organizations protested the crowded and unsanitary conditions in factories and factory dormitories where disease spread rampantly. They argued that the rigors of child labor weakened the future work force; and that at its worst, child labor caused death. They reasoned that children who were working 10-hour days were unfairly denied the universal education promised them by the state.

The tireless efforts of reformers, social workers and unions seemed to pay off in 1916—at the height of the progressive move-

Hine (left) was a key force in exposing the exploitation of children, which included jobs in the garment industry (above) as well as the horrific lot of the breaker boys (opposite page, top) and others forced to work around dangerous machinery; one sad result was children with lost limbs, such as the boy at left.

37

ment—when President Woodrow Wilson passed the Keating-Owen Act banning articles produced by child labor from being sold in interstate commerce. The act was struck down as unconstitutional by the Supreme Court just two years later.

Young girls continued to work in mills, still in danger of slipping and losing a finger or a foot while standing on top of machines to change bobbins; or of being scalped if their hair got caught. And, as ever, after a day of bending over to pick bits of rock from coal, "breaker boys" were still stiff and in pain. If a breaker boy fell, he could still be smothered, or crushed, by huge piles of coal. And, when he turned 12, he would still be forced to go down into the mines and face the threat of cave-ins and explosions.

Indeed, child labor continued unabated until the sweeping Fair Labor Standards Act of 1938 was passed, just two years before Lewis Hine died, and after countless children had fallen prey to disease, injury and premature death.

Aftermath

The Fair Labor Standards Act of 1938 established a minimum wage and limited the age of child laborers to 16 and over, 18 for hazardous occupations. Children 14 and 15 years old were permitted to work in certain occupations after school. Child labor still exists in agriculture, especially among migrant families; and U.S. companies who buy products made by child laborers abroad are often the targets of protest.

Robbed of their youth, children were forced to work wherever the burgeoning American economy needed fodder, in factories (opposite page), fields (above) and sweatshops (top).

WOODROW WILSON

A politician with the soul of the Romantic poets he so admired, Woodrow Wilson possessed an idealism that seems downright quaint in today's cynical political climate. The source of both his greatest accomplishments and his ultimate failure, Wilson's high-minded faith in human nature characterized his leadership of the United States, and indeed the world, through the most uncertain and divisive years of the century.

A quintessential late bloomer, the young Wilson would not have been pegged as the Next Leader of the Free World. He was something of a daydreamer, and he inherited his mother's frail constitution instead of his father's hardy one. He was tall, ungainly and self-conscious, but at the same time possessed a fiery, if unfocused, ambition. As a student at Princeton University, he read voraciously, jotting down favorite passages in a notebook, and eventually discovered his passion for history and politics. Upon graduating in 1879, he enrolled in law school at the University of Virginia, with an eye toward the political arena.

President Woodrow Wilson

"I wish now to record the confession," he wrote from Charlottesville to a friend, "that I am most terribly bored by the noble study of Law sometimes." Nonetheless, he finished his coursework, passed the bar, and opened a practice in Atlanta. Clients stayed away in droves. Wilson eventually returned to school at the age of 26, pursuing his Ph.D. in history and political science at Johns Hopkins University. In 1890, he eagerly accepted a professorship at Princeton, where he would flourish over the next 20 years and find his springboard into politics.

Princeton's Board of Trustees unanimously approved Wilson as the president of the school in 1902. He immediately set about transforming the

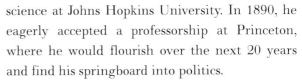

The thoughtful Wilson (left) rose from the presidency of Princeton (top) to the presidency of the entire nation.

41

NO PLACE FOR HER

college into the world-renowned university it is today, presenting a $12.5 million program of innovations. Wilson restructured the faculty, overhauled the curriculum and revised the teaching method. When he tried to reform the eating clubs, which he viewed as a source of campus elitism and alienation, he encountered resistance among powerful alumni. Finally, in 1910, following a bitter controversy over the establishment of the graduate college, Wilson left Princeton, answering the call of the New Jersey Democratic party, whose top brass thought he'd make a viable candidate for governor.

He won the office in 1910, enacting a progressive platform whose success earned him the Democratic presidential nomination just one year later, marking his ascent as one of the most meteoric rises in U.S. political history. After the bluff and bluster of Theodore Roosevelt, the American public was apparently ready for Wilson's fervent idealism and he was elected in a close, three-way election against Republican William Howard Taft and Roosevelt, who mounted a vigorous third-party campaign under the theme of New Nationalism. Wilson wasted no time delivering on his so-called New Freedom platform, passing the Federal Reserve bill in December 1913 to protect the savings of aver-

"There is a great wind of moral force moving through the world, and every man who opposes himself to that wind will go down in disgrace."

—*WOODROW WILSON, 28th U.S. president, 1919*

Wilson's first cabinet (above) included the legendary populist William Jennings Bryan (immediately to Wilson's right); the cartoonists railed about the perils of foreign entanglements (opposite page, left), Wilson himself marched in a Preparedness parade in June 1916 (opposite page) while portraying himself as the man who kept the nation out of war, but in the end the United States had no choice as Wilson stated to Congress in April 1917 in his speech requesting a declaration of war (left).

age Americans just two months after his Underwood Act reformed tariff laws.

The summer of 1914 was a time of upheaval for Wilson as his wife of 29 years, Ellen, died, and war broke out in Europe. Wilson maintained a policy of neutrality, exercising skillful diplomacy with the increasingly hostile British and Germans. Campaigning under the slogan "He Kept us Out of War," Wilson narrowly won reelection in 1916. Soon after the election, however, he no longer found it possible to adhere to that slogan. Germany had stepped up its naval warfare, attacking neutral, commercial vessels as well as hostile ships, and on April 2, 1917, Wilson asked Congress for a declaration of war. He pressured for the Selective Service Act in May of that year, and with the largest armed forces in American history mobilized, the Allies gradually prevailed.

Wilson negotiated the German surrender in the fall of 1918, saying that the settlement would be based on his Fourteen Points, the last of which was the formation of a League of Nations. The following January in Paris, Wilson was a commanding presence at the Peace Conference, pressing the merits of his Fourteen Points and demonstrating keen foresight. The European borders hammered out in the Treaty of Versailles would prove to be more durable than Communism, reemerging intact with the dismantling of the Berlin Wall in 1989.

Wilson threw out the first ball on Opening Day of 1916 (above); a year later the nation was at war and two and a half years later Wilson was traveling to Versailles (top), where he was a towering figure in the peace negotiations; Wilson's efforts to overcome opposition to the League of Nations (opposite page) took its toll, leading to a stroke that left him seriously weakened (opposite page, with his second wife, Edith) by the end of his second term.

OVERWEIGHTED.

PRESIDENT WILSON. "HERE'S YOUR OLIVE BRANCH. NOW GET BUSY."
DOVE OF PEACE. "OF COURSE I WANT TO PLEASE EVERYBODY; BUT ISN'T THIS A BIT THICK?"

Aftermath

Wilson's League of Nations faced tremendous opposition. In response, Wilson embarked on an 8,000-mile tour to stir up public demand for the treaty's ratification. The strain proved costly. Returning to Washington, Wilson suffered a stroke on Oct. 2, 1919, leaving his left side paralyzed for the remainder of his term. The treaty stalemated in Congress, and Wilson's successor in the White House, Warren G. Harding, kept the United States out of the League of Nations. Wilson, who received the Nobel Prize for his efforts in the peace process, retired to a private life in Washington with his second wife, Edith Galt Wilson. He died in 1924.

FUN'S Word-Cross Puzzle.

"Well, I'm going to get you a silver card tray, a bronze statue for the dining room mantlepiece and a new rug to put in front of my dressing table.

"What are you going to do for me?"

"I've been thinking," was the quiet reply, "and I have made up my mind to get you a new shaving brush and a tobacco pouch."

FILL in the small squares with words which agree with the following definitions:

2—3. What bargain hunters enjoy.

4—5. A written acknowledgment.

6—7. Such and nothing more.

10—11. A bird.

14-15. Opposed to less.

18—19. What this puzzle is.

22—23. An animal of prey.

26—27. The close of a day.

28—29. To elude.

30—31. The plural of is.

8—9. To cultivate.

12—13. A bar of wood or iron.

16—17. What artists learn to do.

20—21. Fastened.

24—25. Found on the seashore.

10—18. The fibre of the gomuti palm.

6—22. What we all should be.

4—26. A day dream.

2—11. A talon.

19—28. A pigeon.

F—7. Part of your head.

23—30. A river in Russia.

1—32. To govern.

33—34. An aromatic plant.

N—8. A fist.

24—31. To agree with.

3—12. Part of a ship.

20—29. One.

5—27. Exchanging.

9—25. To sink in mud.

13—21. A boy.

Sour.

"We had four blow-outs on the road last night."

"Your car must be awfully tired."

The Old Suit.

CROSSWORD PUZZLE

It is astonishing what a blank sheet of paper and a looming deadline will do for the imagination.

In 1913, Arthur Wynne, an expatriate Liverpudlian working as an editor at the *New York World*, was racking his brain for a way to spice up the "Fun" section in the Christmas edition of the paper's Sunday magazine. Wynne recalled a Victorian word game called word square that his grandfather had shown him years earlier, in which a list of words had to be arranged in a square so that they read the same horizontally and vertically. After drawing a diamond-shaped grid, Wynne made two key departures from word square. First, he used different words  to fill the vertical and horizontal rows. Then he provided a grid of squares to be filled in. Wynne's new game, which he called "word-cross," made its debut on December 21, 1913.

Readers were so enthusiastic that Wynne decided to make "word-cross" a weekly feature. In its fourth week of existence a typesetter who was either sleepy or dyslexic reversed the two words and gave Wynne's puzzle the name we use to this day.

Wynne began to appreciate the addictive power of his creation when one week he neglected to run a puzzle and was greeted by a blizzard of protest.

For 10 years the *World* was one of the few

To spice up his paper's "Fun" section (left, inset), Wynne created the crossword puzzle (left); soon the craze was on (top).

"Coming up with a new theme for each Sunday's 21-by-21 crossword is no easy matter. O.K., it isn't astrophysics...."

—*Sylvia Bursztyn, co-editor of the Los Angeles Times crossword, 1989*

newspapers to publish crosswords. By 1924 Wynne had moved on, and the daily puzzle was left to a small team of editors that included a young secretary named Margaret Petherbridge, who had been hired partly to weed out the puzzle's many errors. According to a story which, alas, now seems to be apocryphal, Petherbridge took her oath of office with her right hand atop a *Funk & Wagnalls Dictionary*.

In 1924 Richard Simon and Max Schuster, two young Columbia graduates, opened a publishing company and decided, against all advice, to make a collection of crosswords their first offering. Within weeks, the first printing of *The Cross Word Puzzle Book* sold out. So did a second and third. Simon & Schuster, as the two young entrepreneurs had named their company, quickly issued two more volumes of puzzles which, by the end of 1924, stood first, second and third on the national nonfiction bestseller list.

Crossword mania swept the nation. The Baltimore & Ohio Railroad installed dictionaries on its trains, Merriam Webster fell 12 months behind in supplying them, and singer Elsie Janis starred in a critically acclaimed Broadway revue, part of which was set in a "Cross Word Puzzle Sanitorium." (Not a bad idea, although psychologists today believe puzzles may afford a kind of preventive therapy against memory loss in old age.)

The New York Times, which had at first dismissed such puzzle-solving as "a primitive form of mental exercise," finally began publishing crosswords in its Sunday editions beginning in 1942 and in its daily papers in 1950. As its first crossword editor, the *Times* chose—who else?—the former Miss Petherbridge, now Mrs. Farrar, who in her influential 60-year career—27 of those years at the *Times*—helped establish many of the rules that now govern the creation of crosswords: a symmetrical grid design, all-over

48

While Wynne (opposite page) created the first puzzle (with answers filled in, below), Farrar (left) helped establish the crossword as we know it today; at its height, crossword fever even produced popular songs such as the *Cross Word Puzzle Blues* (near left).

interlock, every letter used in an Across and a Down answer, a minimum of black squares, no two-letter words and the livelier the vocabulary the better.

The popularity of the puzzle has spawned a wealth of crossword lore. But the most famous of all crossword stories occurred in 1944, in the weeks leading up to the Normandy invasion. British Intelligence officers were shocked to see words like "Utah" and "Omaha," code names for Normandy beachheads, and "Overlord," the code name for the entire operation, appearing in the *London Daily Telegraph* crossword. Agents rushed to the suburban London home of its creator, Leonard Dawe, and demanded an explanation. Though it turned out to be nothing more than a coincidence, it is not the only time crossword puzzles have seemed like a matter of life and death.

Aftermath

Today the crossword puzzle is the most popular word game in the world. Somewhere between 25 and 30 million Americans do crosswords regularly and perhaps twice that number at least occasionally. They have assumed an importance Arthur Wynne would not have believed. Israeli government censors keep an eye on the crosswords in the Palestinian press, and filmmaker Dusan Makavejev, blacklisted by the Yugoslav government in 1971, claims he knew he was back in good graces when his name appeared in a crossword puzzle.

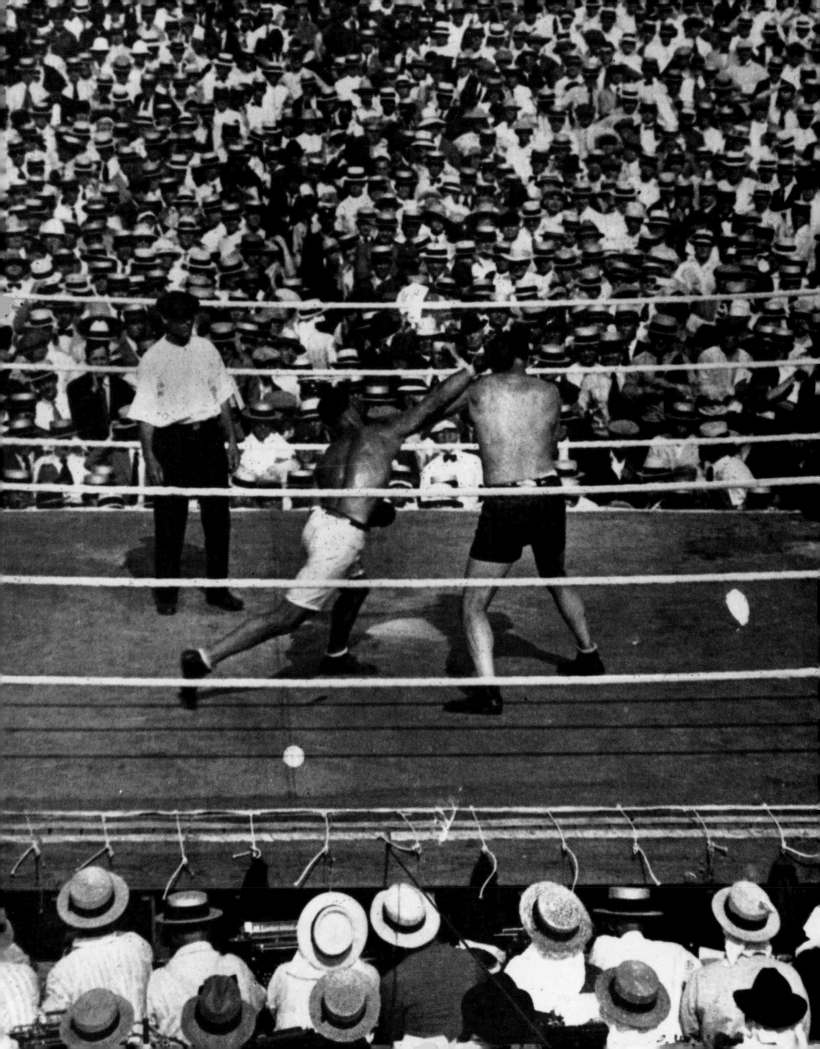

JACK DEMPSEY

With a style forged in the rough and tumble mining towns of Utah and Nevada, Jack Dempsey came East after World War I and bashed his way into American lore. The phrase "killer instinct" entered the language as a reference to the fights that made Dempsey's legend, bruising victories over Jess Willard, Georges Carpentier and Luis Firpo. An icon of America's Golden Age of sport, Dempsey drew the first million-dollar gate in boxing history, and earned handsome sums of up to $300,000 a fight.

His road to these riches was a rough-hewed version of the American Dream. The ninth of 11 children born to an impoverished Scotch-Irish farmworker in Manassa, Colorado, Dempsey left home at 15. He rode the rails and fought, quite literally, for his supper. He lost his share of these unrefereed brawls for pocket change in the copper mines and hobo jungles of the West, but not enough to convince him that working full time in the mines was a more attractive option.

One night, legend has it, Dempsey entered a frontier tavern and found two toughs giving an overmatched out-of-towner a hard time. Dempsey decked the pair, and the man he had protected, one Jack (Doc) Kearns, later telegrammed him in Salt Lake City, urging him to move to Los Angeles to turn professional. Under Kearns's management Dempsey won 69 of 70 bouts, many by devastating knockout. At the age of 24, after demolishing a series of lesser opponents through the earlier years of the decade, Dempsey landed a shot at the heavyweight title, meeting the giant Willard in Toledo, Ohio, on July 4, 1919.

Willard had won the title from Jack Johnson in 1915, knocking out the legendary champion in the 26th—26th!—round in Havana. Willard stood nearly 6 feet 7 inches—more than five inches taller than Dempsey—and weighed 250 pounds. Saying

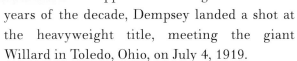

Dempsey (above, on his honeymoon with film star Estelle Taylor) scored early and often against Willard (left).

"You came out of a fight with Dempsey full of welts and bruises and every bone aching."

—*JACK SHARKEY, heavyweight who lost to Dempsey in 1927*

"I outweigh him by 70 pounds," Willard entered the ring overconfident and undertrained. He left it with a broken jaw, one eye swollen shut, two broken ribs, and six teeth broken off at the gums. In a savaging that could never occur under today's rules, Willard was floored seven times in the first round alone, as Dempsey stood over him, pounding Willard each time the big man attempted to rise. Astonishingly, Willard lasted through the third round.

Promoter Tex Rickard built a huge outdoor stadium in Jersey City, New Jersey, for Dempsey's fight with Carpentier, a French war hero and the champion of Europe. The so-called "Battle of the Century" attracted more than 80,000 fans and grossed $1,789,238, but the fight failed to live up to its billing as the Manassa Mauler dropped Gorgeous Georges in four. Dempsey's next big bout came against the massive Firpo of Argentina. The 125,000 spectators crammed into New York's Polo Grounds witnessed one of the more memorable slugfests in boxing history. Staggered in the opening exchange, Dempsey recovered to floor Firpo five times. After the fifth knockdown, Firpo got up, charged Dempsey and, pinning him against the ropes, connected with a thunderous right. Dempsey landed in the front row. According to one account, the dazed champion asked his corner at the break, "Which round was I knocked out in?" Informed he was still in the fight, Dempsey decked Firpo twice in Round 2, the second time for good.

Dempsey (above) met his match in the less devastating but more skilled Tunney (above, at right in ring) who defeated him twice; after his marriage to Taylor, Dempsey's relationship to his manager, Kearns (left), deteriorated badly, leaving him less than sharp for his first bout with Tunney.

The fight against Carpentier (top) attracted some 80,000 fans to the stadium Rickard constructed in Jersey City; after the fact, Rickard made still **more money on the filmed version of the fight (above); away from all the tumult, Dempsey (right) liked to relax and read in his rocking chair.**

Dempsey's marriage to film star Estelle Taylor eventually fractured his partnership with Kearns, and the ensuing lawsuits delayed any title defenses. Finally, in September 1926, he met Gene Tunney in Philadelphia. The layoff showed: Dempsey lost a 10-round decision. He appeared on the verge of regaining the title when he met Tunney again, in Chicago, on Sept. 22, 1927, and flattened him with a combination of hooks in the seventh round. As Dempsey stood over the vanquished Tunney, referee Dave

Barry, in accordance with the new rules, motioned Dempsey to the neutral corner, delaying his count until the fighter obeyed the order. Observers estimated that Tunney was on the canvas for 14 seconds, but by Barry's count, he got up at nine. He recovered to outpoint Dempsey again.

Tunney claimed that he could have risen by nine even without the benefit of the now famous "long count." When told of this Dempsey, ever the gentleman, replied, "If that's what Gene says, "I will not doubt his word."

Aftermath

Dempsey retired after the second Tunney fight, then made a brief, unsuccessful comeback four years later. He sparred with future champions Max Schmeling and Max Baer in the 1930s, when he also trained "Two Ton" Tony Galento for a short time. In 1936, he opened Jack Dempsey's restaurant in New York City and operated the business for the next 37 years. During WWII he served as a physical education instructor in the Coast Guard. He died in 1983 at the age of 88.

CONSTRUCTION TOYS

Toys—like art, music and literature—are expressions of their times. Hence it is no surprise that a new era of skyscrapers, airplanes and automobiles could no longer make do with the rocks, sticks, corn cobs and pine cones that had served as building toys from time immemorial. Sure, alphabet blocks were fine for learning to read and spell but they limited the imagination of the construction-minded child to the simplest towers. And, yes, with a set of colored stone Richter Anchor Blocks, a child could make various types of buildings such as castles with turrets and towers. But how could children destined to lead the nation into the glittering new century be limited to the less than spectacular heights dictated by gravity?

Thus, when structural steel was introduced at the end of the nineteenth century, it not only inspired architects to build upward and transform American cities, but also made way for a new generation of forward-looking toys, such as the Erector® Set, first sold in 1913, that would encourage families and children to make good use of their new-found leisure time. By 1904, the American Art Stone and Manufacturing Company had added "steel beams" to stone blocks so children too could build skyscrapers. Five years later, they could learn basic engineering by making Ferris wheels, windmills and bridges with Kilbourn's Construction Strips.

But the toy that galvanized families across the nation—especially fathers and sons—and epito-

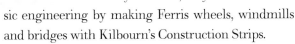

Construction sets like Structo's (top) allowed kids to build astonishingly complex edifices like the one at left.

"I'll tell you boys, being an engineer is the most exciting thing in the world. And that's just what you are when you have one of my new Erectors®."
—A.C. GILBERT, *Erector® Set inventor*

mized the nation's growing interest in educational pastimes was the Erector® Set. The creator of this modern marvel was Alfred Carlton Gilbert, an Olympic gold medal-winning pole vaulter, doctor from Yale and inveterate purveyor of magic tricks. While traveling by train from New Haven, Connecticut, to New York City, Gilbert caught sight of steel girders being erected to carry electrical lines for trains and conceived the notion that a toy that allowed kids to capture that creative spirit might just be successful. After several years of build-

ing prototypes, he unveiled his sets of metal strips, nuts, bolts, gears and pinions to immediate success among buyers at the 1913 New York City toy show.

The largest sets came in wooden chests with drawers and included electric motors that required assembly. Instruction manuals had pictures of the various designs but no step-by-step directions for constructing even the most complex cars, buildings, drawbridges and air compressors. That was left to the child's imagination and ingenuity.

After only one year on the market, Erector®

While there were numerous competing products such as the American Model Builder (above), Gilbert's Erector® Sets, with their signature "Hello Boys!" ad slogan (right), clearly led the field; Lincoln Logs (below) were a favorite of the younger crowd.

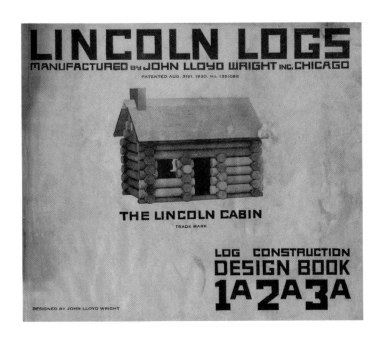

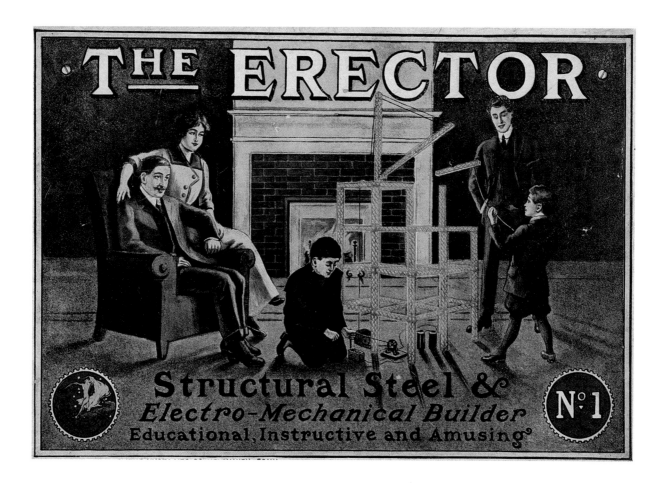

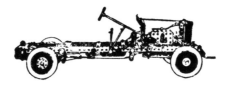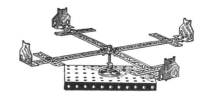

Erector® Sets allowed
for the construction of
an array of products;
they even helped ensure
domestic tranquillity
(opposite page).

drew more than 60,000 children to participate in its first annual Erector® model building contest. Other makes, such as Meccano, American Model Builder and Structo Building Sets brought competition to the market. But with its reasonable prices, national advertising and superior design, Erector® prevailed. Of course there were other products for the less advanced—while older boys and their fathers built derricks and ship cranes with their Erector® Sets, younger children played with Tinker Toys (1914), the idea for which came to Charles Pajeau while he watched a child poke sticks into the holes of thread spools.

If Erector® Sets helped children prepare for the future, then Lincoln Logs, the era's other most popular construction toy, taught them to appreciate the wilderness they were moving farther and farther away from. Although there was an earlier version called Log Cabin Playhouses (1866), the toy as we know it was invented by John Lloyd Wright, son of the famous architect Frank Lloyd Wright. In 1915, the younger Wright was inspired by the floating cantilever construction his father used in Tokyo's Imperial Hotel.

At a time of increasing urbanization, these simple notched hardwood logs offered the comfort of

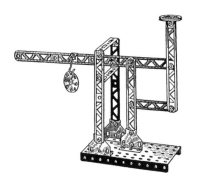

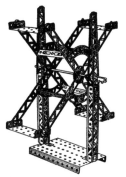

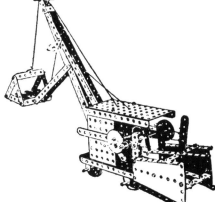

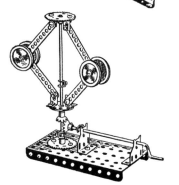

nostalgia. Writers and illustrators were touting the spirit of frontier life; the camping movement had taken hold among middle-class youth; and Lincoln Logs quickly achieved mass appeal. Because they came in varying sizes, they required skill and attention in construction as well as repacking, thus satisfying the public appetite for toys that encouraged analytical development.

Born from an increase in family leisure time, a fascination with things mechanical, and a belief that even playtime should contribute to civilization, construction toys were indeed an apt symbol of a nation in transition.

Aftermath

More than 10 million sets of Lincoln Logs have been sold since 1915. And although plastic versions have been introduced, the original wooden logs are still made at a factory in Walla Walla, Washington. By the time of A.C. Gilbert's retirement in 1956, more than 40 million Erector® Sets had been sold, making them one of the world's most popular toys. When the A.C. Gilbert Company was broken up in the mid-60s, however, the Erector® trademark was sold to Gabriel Industries. It later went to Tyco and finally to Meccano, Erector's® longtime competitor, which reintroduced Erector® Sets to the American market after a 10-year absence. LEGO is the leading construction toy on the market today, followed by K'Nex.

THE FEDERAL RESERVE ACT

Great economies surge and recede like the sea. They are lifted by the high tides of prosperity and they fall in times of panic. Provided they are not too extreme, such shifts are normal features of economic growth, especially when a country is expanding the way the United States was at the turn of the century. In both 1893 and 1895 the U.S. economy had experienced tremors of anxiety. Each time it weathered them, doing so in 1895 with the help of financial titan J.P. Morgan, who put together a syndicate of bankers that bailed out the government with a loan of 3.5 million ounces of gold.

But the great banking crisis of 1907 was different from its predecessors. It was bigger and therefore scarier. Once more, Treasury officials called upon Morgan for help, but this time even he could not raise enough money to save the country. In fact, Morgan had to turn to Washington for help. In the short run the crisis resulted in the closing of The Knickerbocker Trust Company, the third largest bank in New York; in the long run it forced the U.S. government to confront the dangers inherent in its banking system. It produced the single most important piece of legislation of Woodrow Wilson's two terms, the Federal Reserve Act of 1913, which, despite some modifications over the years, constitutes the system we use today.

The crisis of 1907 also fanned the flames of populist indignation, for it reminded working people where power really lay. In one way, of course, it was kind of Morgan and his friends to bail out the country. But once the rescue had been made, it was impossible for ordinary folks to forget what they had just witnessed: One man had enough money and influence to save an entire country! And what power Morgan didn't have, his cronies

The crisis of 1907 led to panic on Wall Street (left) and a run on various banks, such as New York's Lincoln Trust (top).

in New York seemed to. The fear that a small "money trust," controlled the U.S. economy spread rapidly, reaching a fever pitch in 1912 when a House banking subcommittee revealed that 12 big banks in New York, Boston and Chicago controlled an inordinate number of corporations.

By 1910, when the populist Democrats regained control of Congress, virtually everyone agreed the system would have to be changed. The only question was how.

Leading the Republicans was Nelson Aldrich, the patrician U.S. senator from Rhode Island. In 1910 Aldrich invited some of the most powerful men on Wall Street to Jekyll Island, off the coast of Georgia, to draw up plans for a national banking system. Knowing full well how such a meeting would be viewed by the public and especially by the Democrats, Aldrich and his associates kept it

secret. They proposed a network of 15 regional banks whose decisions would be overseen by a central board of commercial bankers. The Aldrich Plan was rejected by the House and the issue remained unresolved until Woodrow Wilson was sworn in as president in 1913.

Though Wilson was a Democrat, he too believed something had to be done about the "money trust" problem: "A concentration of the control of credit may at any time become infinitely dangerous to freedom," he said in accepting the Democratic nomination in the summer of 1912. What Wilson envisioned was a system very much like the one proposed by Aldrich and his cohorts—a network of regional banks overseen by a central governing board. What was radical then, and continues to be the model for liberal democracies today, was that the system would have both public and private as-

As the cartoons on the opposite page suggest, Congress had to be pressured into passing Wilson's reform, while the cities hoping for regional banks couldn't see it passed quickly enough; the final plan was similar to that proposed by Aldrich (right), with the critical difference being the inclusion of a public governing board in Wilson's version.

"The house of Morgan towered above the pedestrian ranks of American finance and business like a great baronial castle, dreadful in its feudal power but also admirable in its way."

—*WILLIAM GREIDER, in "Secrets of the Temple: How the Federal Reserve Runs the Country" (1987)*

pects. As drafted by Congressman Carter Glass of Virginia and Senator Robert Owen of Oklahoma, the legislation addressed three key problems. First, it spread reserves more evenly throughout the country by establishing a network of 12 regional reserve banks, which answered to a Board appointed by the president and confirmed by the Senate; second, it fortified banks in the South and West, where most of the shortages had occurred; and finally, it established an "elastic" currency that would grow or shrink according to credit demands. While populists complained that the Federal Reserve Act was a sellout to Wall Street, Wall Street would certainly have preferred a system that was completely private. But the bill passed the House by a vote of 298 to 60, and the Senate by 43 to 25. On December 23, 1913, President Wilson signed the Federal Reserve Act into law.

Aftermath

If you're looking for proof of the Federal Reserve Board's continuing power, consider how the stock market reacts every time Chairman Alan Greenspan announces a change in the interest rate or makes a comment that might imply a change, as in his 1997 congressional testimony suggesting that the U.S. stock market was in the throes of "irrational exuberance." Or consider the conspiracy theorists who insist that the Act was passed illegally, in the dead of night, when its tired opponents in Congress had gone home—a theory whose tenacity seems to bear no relation to its utter falsehood.

THE GRAND CANYON

Poets, artists and adventurers alike testify daily to the natural world's power to touch the soul and stir the imagination. Yet when army lieutenant Joseph Ives led a survey party through the Grand Canyon in 1857, this majestic world wonder, designated a National Park in 1919, registered a loathsome blip on his emotional radar screen. "The region," he wrote, "is of course altogether valueless. Ours has been the first, and will doubtless be the last, party of whites to visit this profitless locality."

Grand Canyon National Park 1919

Perhaps Ives had not seen the 277-mile-long canyon just before dusk, when the sun's sinking rays set fire to the millions of layers of limestone, shale, granite and sandstone that make up the canyon's towering walls. Or maybe he had slept through the pastel blues, purples and gold of early morning.

It is true that the canyon's south rim, from which his party set out, is mostly desert, and hos- pitable to little flora—other than the Piñon Pine, Utah Juniper, various cacti and yucca—and to still less fauna—mainly the Abert squirrel and rock pocket mouse. But it is also the gateway to a magnificent "geological textbook" in which each exposed layer of earth is like a page describing the earth's history. The oldest rock, at Inner Gorge, dates back more than two billion years, to when the plateau through which the Colorado River now cuts was just beginning to form.

In all fairness to the near-sighted lieutenant, this winding stretch of rapid-filled river, sunk a mile deep into a rocky plateau in northeast Arizona, had also failed to inspire kind words from Spaniards searching for gold in the 1500s and from American trappers 300 years later. Even Major John Wesley Powell, a fearless, one-armed Civil War veteran who, in 1869, led a party of nine down

Since the second Powell expedition (top), millions of visitors have witnessed the grandeur of the Grand Canyon (left).

the then uncharted Colorado referred to the mile-high canyon walls as "our granite prison" in a moment of despair. After becoming the first white man to explore the entire length of the canyon, Powell returned for a second expedition literally to put the Grand Canyon on the map. Fortune-seeking prospectors followed close on his heels, but at least two were driven away in 1874 by hostile Indians, possibly related to the ones who had claimed three of Powell's men, believing the soldiers had killed women of their tribe.

Native Americans had been inhabiting the canyon for as many as 5,000 years, judging from twig animal figurines discovered in Luka Cave in 1933 and attributed to the Pinto-Basin Desert Culture. By 1100 A.D., hundreds of Anasazi Indians—consummate basket weavers—farmed the canyon and rim along with the Cohonina Tribe. The lack of rainfall may have driven both tribes from the canyon in 1150, but it was soon repopulated by Cerbats—ancestors of the Havasupai and the Hualapai, among the only Native Americans now living in the canyon.

That the white man had granted more than two centuries of tranquillity to Native Americans in the canyon spoke less of his humanity than of the extreme difficulties in exploring, let alone inhabiting it. But once interest in the canyon took hold, stagecoach lines and accommodations were

The breathtaking views, put on the white man's map by Powell (opposite page), included the view of the Colorado River, 3,000 feet below the rim (above) and majestic limestone pinnacles (left); the canyon's increasing popularity led to slides of its vistas for stereoscopes (opposite page, top).

"The most impressive piece of scenery I have ever looked at...It is beautiful and terrible and unearthly... Leave it as it is. You cannot improve on it."

—*President Theodore Roosevelt, 1903*

quickly established. And on December 19, 1901, the first train on the Santa Fe line rolled up to the canyon's rim.

Convinced of the Grand Canyon's significance as a natural attraction and tourist destination, the senator from Indiana, Benjamin Harrison, lobbied hard but unsuccessfully for the establishment of "The National Park of the Grand Cañon of the Colorado" in 1886. Seven years later, as president, Harrison created the Great Canyon Reserve, a move opposed by local inhabitants who resented government control of their land and claims. In 1906, President Theodore Roosevelt, who was fond of hunting among the evergreen

stands and grasslands of the canyon's north rim, created the Grand Canyon Game Preserve, and then in 1908, the Grand Canyon National Monument. By the time Arizona received statehood in 1912, residents had recognized the tremendous benefits of having a national park within their borders. On February 26, 1919, President Woodrow Wilson signed the Grand Canyon National Park Act to create the seventeenth of today's 25 national parks. In the 140 years following Lieutenant Ives's flawed prediction, so many visitors have peered in wonder from the edge of the park's major overlooks that in many spots the stone has been worn smooth.

Aftermath

In 1919, the year of its formation, the Grand Canyon National Park received 44,000 visitors. Since that time, annual visitation has steadily climbed, to 106,000 in 1915 and more than a million by 1956; two million by 1969; three million by 1976; four million by 1992; and, only one year later, just short of five million—a number that remains the norm today. Until the 1920s the average visitor to the Grand Canyon stayed two or three weeks. A typical visit these days lasts two or three hours.

Through the years, outings such as the one on the opposite page have become more and more common; whether in temperate weather (top) or bedecked in snow (above), the canyon offers visitors a plethora of stunning views.

Panama Canal

The challenge was enormous, the reward great. For centuries, rulers had dreamed of carving a waterway between the Atlantic and Pacific Oceans that would enable ships to avoid the 9,000-mile journey around South America's treacherous Cape Horn. Until the first vessel traversed the Panama Canal in 1914, however, that goal had been fanciful at best. Standing in the way of its realization were herculean obstacles, most notably the Culebra mountain range that divides the Panamanian isthmus. "What God has joined together, let no man put asunder," warned seventeenth-century advisers to King Phillip II of Spain, a maxim that effectively expressed the sentiment of numerous leaders who had considered then rejected the dangerous undertaking.

This negativism, of course, was not in keeping with the can-do spirit of the modern industrial age. And so, in 1881, a French company undertook the project. But Ferdinand de Lesseps, head of the Compagnie Universelle du Canal Interocéanique, grossly underestimated the challenge of the Culebras, not to mention the difficulties resulting from a wet jungle climate that caused iron and steel to rust in a matter of days and the most deadly enemies of all, yellow fever and malaria. After eight years, the French abandoned their power shovels, dredges and locomotives. The project's toll: 20,000 lives lost and $287 million down the drain.

Undaunted by the French fiasco, Theodore Roosevelt pushed for a Central American canal even before he became president. He had watched with dismay as the USS *Oregon*, dispatched to Cuba at the onset of the Spanish-American War in 1898, had taken 67 days to travel from San Francisco. In his view and the view of others, the navy had to be more mobile if the United States was to establish and

The ingenious system of locks (top) allowed ships to be lifted and lowered (left) on their way from sea to sea.

73

"No single great material work which remains to be under-taken on this continent is of such consequence to the American people."

—*THEODORE ROOSEVELT,*
26th U.S. president, 1902

Two years after his Secretary of the Treasury, Leslie Shaw, signed the Panama Canal agreement in 1904 (above), Theodore Roosevelt paid a visit to Panama (left); the foot gate of the Gatun Locks (opposite page) was an enormous undertaking—once built, water was pumped in or out of the locks (opposite page, below) to enable ships' passage.

maintain its influence overseas and particularly within its own hemisphere.

In 1899, the United States purchased the rights to build a canal from the French for $40 million and Congress established the Isthmian Canal Commission. When the Colombian government, which controlled Panama, held out for more money, Roosevelt—in a typical example of gunboat diplomacy—backed Panama's successful drive for independence. Then, for $10 million up front and $250,000 annually in perpetuity, the United States bought the Canal Zone, a 10-by-40-mile swath of mountainous jungle connecting the Atlantic and Pacific Oceans.

Work on the canal began mid-year 1904. A year later morale had reached an alltime low as workers confronted poor housing, terrible food, illness and boredom. When Roosevelt's first chief engineer, John F. Wallace, resigned in June 1905, Roosevelt dispatched a new appointee, John Frank Stevens, with a warning that he would find "a devil of a mess." And Stevens did. The port cities were filthy, the drinking water bad. Arcane government regulations prohibited carpenters from cutting a board longer than 10 feet without a written permit and required that six documents be signed to obtain a handcart.

Culebra Cut from Contractor's Hill, Panama Canal.

Reporting directly to the president, Stevens halted work on the Culebra Cut—the canal's most critical element—and launched a campaign to shore up worker morale. Swamps were drained and pesticides sprayed to eliminate disease, roads were paved and plumbing was installed. Entire towns rose from the jungle, complete with churches, commissaries, decent housing, schools and hospitals.

Then Stevens made a decision that proved critical to the realization of the project. He abandoned the idea of a sea-level canal—that some of the French too had favored—and lobbied Washington instead on behalf of a system of locks which, he argued, would be safer, require less time and energy to build and would cost less to operate and maintain. The end result would be a

process that literally lifted ships up and over the mountains. On June 21, 1906, Congress voted 36 to 31 in favor of the lock canal. A dam would transform the wild Chagres River into the Gatun Lake and a series of locks would raise ships to its level for passage through the Culebra Cut.

Although Stevens stayed on the job only until 1907, his ingenious system of rail transportation in which 30 trains moved in and out of the Culebra Cut every hour with hundreds of tracks being shifted every two to three days became the backbone of a system that allowed his successor, the supremely organized and effective Colonel George Washington Goethals, to steer the project to completion.

On May 20, 1913, the nine-mile-long Culebra Cut was finished. Dynamite, rock drills, a fleet

The Culebra Cut (opposite page) was nine miles in length and had an average depth of 120 feet; huge steam shovels (above) and dredgers (above, right) were used for the task of moving earth and water; Stevens's efforts boosted the spirits of the workers (right) considerably.

of 68 steam shovels weighing as much as 95 tons apiece and a crew of 6,000 men had worked seven days a week for seven years to remove hundreds of millions of cubic yards of earth, which was then carried by train to be used as fill for swamps and at the Gatun dam site. Finally, on January 7, 1914, a crane boat made the first complete passage from the Atlantic to the Pacific side. The Panama Canal had been completed six months ahead of schedule, despite delays from landslides, and at a total cost to the United States of $352 million, $23 million under budget.

The realization of a centuries-old dream and arguably the greatest engineering project in history, however, was back page news. German troops were marching across Belgium toward Paris.

Aftermath

Traffic through the canal was light during WWI. But since 1960, the canal has been handling 12,000 to 15,000 ships annually, or about 50 ships a day. The average length of transit is eight hours, the average toll $16,000. Following years of negotiations, new treaties between the United States and Panama were signed in 1979, turning the administration of the Canal Zone over to Panama. The United States will cede operating control of the canal to Panama by December 31, 1999.

SCOUTING

According to the second edition of the *Random House Unabridged Dictionary*, a scout is "a person sent out to obtain information"; and to scout is "to examine, inspect, or observe for the purpose of obtaining information." Although most commonly used as a military term, the word scout—from the French "écouter," or listen—has made literary appearances as far back as Shakespeare. It was also frequently used in American records of the Indian wars. And, from time immemorial, it has identified the servants of Oxford undergraduates.

When, in 1907, British army officer and war hero Robert S.S. Baden-Powell began a new camping movement for boys in England—called Boy Scouts—the word "scout" took on new meaning. No longer simply a military term for a man trained in re-

connaissance, the word scout connoted qualities of resourcefulness, adaptability, leadership and, most of all, strong moral fiber. Explaining his choice of the name "Boy Scouts," Baden-Powell said: "With a view to making the subject appeal to boys and to meet their spirit of adventure, I hold up for their ideal the doings of backwoodsmen and knights, adventurers and explorers as the heroes for them to follow. These I group generally under the title of Scout."

The Boy Scouts was not the only, or even the first, outdoors organization for boys at the beginning of the twentieth century. But it did have several distinctive features, such as the uniform, the Motto, the Scout Oath and the Good Turn, which contributed to its instant popularity among youth and adults. Baden-Powell had

Begun in 1910 and 1912 respectively, the Boy Scouts (left) and the Girl Scouts (top) have become enormously popular.

> **"In those days, girls were supposed to knit and sew and be nice and clean. Scouting gave us a cross-section of exciting things to explore."**
>
> —*SYLVIA RADOV, 81, former scout, retired librarian, 1997*

worn a uniform his entire adult life and knew how much it could do for a boy's sense of belonging and purpose. The "Be Prepared" motto meant that a Scout should be ready to help other people at all times, maybe even save a life by applying first aid. It was a new concept brimming with educational and social appeal. The Scout Oath, or promise, was the boy's pledge to do his best to live up to the scout laws, which Baden-Powell based on the Code of Chivalry of the Knights of the Middle Ages. Modern-day Scouts were to be loyal, trustworthy, courteous and kind. They were also to do a Good Turn daily. It was this last commitment that was responsible for bringing the Boy Scouts to the United States.

As the story goes, an eager Scout helped William D. Boyce, a Chicago publisher in London on business, find his way through a thick fog. When Boyce offered a shilling for his help, the boy turned it down saying, "Sir, I thank you. I am a Scout. A Scout does not accept tips for courtesies and Good Turns." That very day, the Scout introduced Boyce to Baden-Powell. The former returned to the United States with literature, insignia, and uniforms and on February 8, 1910, the "Boy Scouts of America" was incorporated in the District of Columbia.

The outdoors movement—a healthful antidote to growing industrialization—had reached an alltime high in the United States, and by November 10 of that year, the Boy Scouts of America had absorbed more than a half-dozen similar organizations into

80

As envisioned by Baden-Powell (opposite page, bottom) and Low (opposite page, top), the scouting life included such practical matters as learning first aid (right and above) as well as more lighthearted enterprises such as building tree houses (left).

its ranks. Even before a national campaign could be organized, Scout Troups with volunteer Scoutmasters and Patrol Leaders were popping up across the country. The national character of the organization was underscored when President William Howard Taft, the organization's honorary president, hosted the first annual meeting of the Boy Scouts of America at the White House on February 14 and 15, 1911. In just one year, the organization had attracted 61,495 Scouts and Scoutmasters.

Oddly enough, the overwhelming popularity of the Boy Scouts of America did not immediately generate a similar movement among girls. Those seeds would have to be imported and sewn by Juliette Gordon Low, who had learned of Lord Baden-Powell's Girl Guide movement while living in Scotland in 1911. After returning to the States, Low organized the first American Girl Guides in Savannah, Georgia, on March 12, 1912. It counted 18 members. A year later, the name was changed to Girl Scouts and headquarters were opened in the nation's capital.

By the end of the decade, 1.3 million boys and more than 52,000 girls had taken the oath to live by the definition of the word "scout" as spelled out in Scout Law.

© REINTHAL & NEWMAN. PUBS. N.Y.

Aftermath

The Boy Scouts of America now counts more than 4.4 million youth members, and the Girl Scouts 3.3 million. Globally, the organizations number in the tens of millions. More than 22 million copies of *The Boy Scout Handbook*, a training manual, have been printed since 1910. While camping, hiking and singing continue to be integral activities among Scouts, members are just as likely to work on computers, help the homeless and explore career aptitudes and opportunities. As a recent recruitment poster for the Girl Scouts summer camp states, "It's a great résumé builder."

The outdoors movement motivated the Scouts to learn the basics of camping, including knot making (opposite page, left), living in tents (opposite page) and cooking al fresco (top); the ideal of youth projected by the Scouts (above) persists to this day.

TRANSCONTINENTAL TELEPHONE

Wendover, Utah, is a speck on the map, resembling nothing so much as the last stop before the end of the world. You know you are in the middle of nowhere when the nearest town, 40 miles away, is called Oasis.

Wendover is also the closest town to the famed Salt Flats, where for years men have pushed the land-speed record faster and faster, which seems appropriate, since it was there, on July 28, 1914, that mass communication went into hyperdrive. On that day, the last pole of the transcontinental phone line was erected. A year later Alexander Graham Bell placed the ceremonial first transcontinental telephone call, from New York City to San Francisco, where his assistant, Thomas Watson, was waiting. Their conversation alluded humorously to their historic first phone call 39 years earlier.

"Mr. Watson, come here," said Bell. "I want you."

To which the trusty Watson replied, "Sorry, Mr. Bell. I can't. I'm too far away."

Obviously, it is impossible to evaluate in any precise way how much the world's great inventions have transformed our lives. But Bell's telephone must rank near the top. Indeed, of the five major "domestic" technologies that entered the consumer mainstream in the first half of this century (the others being the electric light, the automobile, the radio and the television), the telephone was the first to be used on a mass scale, with more than 25 percent of American households owning one by 1910. Though just more than a million were in operation at the turn of the century, by 1915 that number topped 10 million.

Bell was born in Edinburgh, Scotland, in 1847 to a family of speech and communication theorists and teachers. His grandfather, who also was named Alexander Bell, was a superb orator and student of

By 1923, with the wiring of the nation well under way (top), phone booths were a common sight in New York City (left).

The advent of the telephone quickly led to the need for switchboards (left), a major source of employment for women in the '20s and '30s; at the San Francisco end of the first transcontinental call, the mayor of San Francisco (above, with phone in front of him) participated along with Watson (to his left).

what today is called speech therapy. His second son, Melville, shared his fascination with speech and hearing problems, an interest that deepened when he married Eliza Grace Symonds, a deaf woman 10 years his senior who inspired all who met her by becoming an accomplished pianist.

Their son inherited the family interest in speech, sound and the problems of the deaf. A modest man who once said he'd rather be remembered for teaching the deaf than inventing the telephone, Bell moved to Canada in 1870 to recover from tuberculosis, which had claimed the lives of both his brothers. He wound up teaching at the Boston School for the Deaf, where he met both the woman who would become his wife, Mabel Hubbard, and

Watson, who he soon discovered shared his interest in the physics of sound.

Bell had always been an enthusiastic inventor, and spent much of his spare time in Boston working on two devices. One he called a "harmonic telegraph," a device for transmitting multiple telegraph signals simultaneously. The other was a machine to record sound waves graphically. By 1874, the two ideas were beginning to merge in Bell's mind. He argued that if he could "make a current of electricity vary in intensity precisely as the air varies in density during the production of sound," he could "transmit speech telegraphically." On March 7, 1876, Bell was issued U.S. patent number 174,465 for his telephone, and three days later he made the historic first call to Watson. In May of 1876, the telephone made its debut at the Philadelphia Centennial Exposition, where it shocked the Brazilian emperor. "My God!" he exclaimed. "It talks!"

Bell made a bold prediction. "It is conceivable," he said, "that cables of telephone

The early phones invented by Bell (above) were all of the type shown at right, with the speaking device attached to the base of the telephone, rather than being paired with the earpiece in a single unit.

"My! How sweet and clear my daughter's voice sounds! She seems to be right here with me."

—*FROM A 1915 ADVERTISEMENT PROMOTING TELEPHONE USE*

wires could be laid underground, or suspended overhead, communicating with private dwellings, country houses, shops, manufactories, etc., etc., uniting them through the main cable with a central office where the wires could be connected as desired, establishing direct communication between any two places in the city."

It was astonishing how quickly Bell's vision became reality. On January 28, 1878, the first commercial telephone exchange was established in New Haven, Connecticut, with 21 subscribers. That same year Rutherford B. Hayes became the first president to use a telephone, and Theodore N. Vail took over the operation of the Bell Company, turning it into the world's most powerful utility. By 1890 telephone networks were all over New England. By 1893 they had reached Chicago, by 1897 Texas. By 1904 telephones were ringing all over the country. They continued to do so until August 4, 1922, when the the nation observed a minute of silence to honor their inventor, who had died two days earlier in Nova Scotia.

Aftermath

In the ensuing years, the reach of the telephone expanded. The first transatlantic call was successfully completed in 1926, and residential service existed in more than 50 percent of all U.S. homes by 1946. On November 18, 1955, the nation's 50-millionth telephone was installed, on President Dwight Eisenhower's desk. Bell's family name lived on in the company that he founded and from which his heirs continued to draw a significant income. The first touchtone phone appeared in 1963; cordless and cellular models followed in 1967 and 1983 respectively.

Early switchboards (opposite page, left) soon gave way to the much more sophisticated centers (opposite page, right) needed to handle long-distance and transcontinental calls; phone booths were sometimes placed in unusual spots (left); telephones installed on the farm (above) helped to lessen the rural population's sense of isolation.

JIM THORPE

"Sir, you are the greatest athlete in the world," said King Gustav V of Sweden to the broad-shouldered young man standing before him. To which Jim Thorpe replied, "Thanks, King." The year was 1912, the place Stockholm's red-brick Olympic stadium, and King Gustav was unwittingly launching a debate that has continued to engage kings and commoners, barons and barflies, ever since: Who is the greatest athlete in history? Is it Michael Jordan? Jesse Owens? Jim Brown? Perhaps Deion Sanders? How about Dan O'Brien, the 1996 Olympic decathlon champion?

In 1950, when the Associated Press asked a group of sportswriters from around the country to name the greatest athlete of the first half of the twentieth century, their answer was Thorpe, the astonishingly versatile Native American who not only won the Olympic decathlon, but also is enshrined in both the college and pro football Halls of Fame and batted .252 in seven seasons of major league baseball. In 1912—a good year if ever there was one—Thorpe won two Olympic gold medals, was named All America at halfback and won the intercollegiate ballroom dancing championship.

Thorpe was born in 1888 on a farm near Prague, Oklahoma, where his father, Hiram, supported his wife and 11 children by breeding and training horses. Thorpe's mother, who like her husband was part Indian, gave him the Indian name Wa-Tho-Huck, which means "Bright Path." But Thorpe's path in life was anything but bright. When Thorpe was 10, his beloved twin brother, Charles, died of pneumonia, leaving him with a profound sense of loneliness that would haunt him the rest of his life. His mother died when he was 12, his father three years later. Indeed, his story is poignant in part because his fall in later life from fame to poverty and obscurity

Thorpe (left, competing in the javelin) proudly marched in the opening ceremonies with the U.S. team (top).

91

"The modern-day Olympics started in 1896, and they had no hard-and-fast rules on mixing professional and amateur sports. They sort of made the rules on Dad."
—*THORPE'S DAUGHTER GRACE, 1995*

Among the events in
which Thorpe competed
for his gold medals were
the discus (left)—he won
the competition in both
the decathlon and the
pentathlon—and
the 200-meter run
(opposite page), which
was only contested in the
pentathlon and which
Thorpe also won.

yards for a touchdown against Army only to have the play called back because of a penalty. On the next play Thorpe ran 97 yards for another touchdown. He won All America honors at halfback in both 1911 and 1912, and later, as a professional, led the Canton Bulldogs to league titles in 1916, 1917 and 1919.

But the 1912 Olympic Games were Thorpe's greatest stage. He won the pentathlon first, then finished fourth in the open high jump and seventh in the open long jump. Finally, in the decathlon, Thorpe amassed a world record of 8,412 points finishing 688 points ahead of the silver medalist—the second largest margin in Olympic decathalon history! Along with his gold medals, he was given a life-size bronze bust of King Gustav and a bejeweled replica of a Viking ship. Back home, he was honored with a ticker-tape parade down Broadway.

But Thorpe did not enjoy his celebrity for long. In January of 1913 it was revealed that in the summers of 1909 and 1910 he had been paid $25 a week to play minor league baseball in North Carolina. Under the strict rules of amateurism, he had been ineligible to compete in Stockholm and was forced to return his medals. "Rules are like steamrollers," Thorpe once wrote. "There is nothing they won't do to flatten the man who stands in their way."

During the Depression Thorpe drifted from job to job, working as a day-laborer on construction sites, a bouncer and even as an extra in Hollywood Westerns. In 1932, when the Olympic Games came to Los Angeles, where Thorpe was living, he could not even afford tickets. Vice President Charles Cur-

calls to mind the woes his people have experienced in America.

In 1904 Thorpe decided to pursue his first love, football, at the Indian Industrial School in Carlisle, Pennsylvania, where the legendary Pop Warner was coach. Once he reached his adult size in 1908, he became a terror on the gridiron. It was not unusual for him to have a hand (or foot!) in all of his team's points. In 1911 Carlisle shocked top-ranked Harvard 18–15 with Thorpe kicking four field goals, an extra point and scoring a touchdown (then worth five points). In 1912 he ran 92

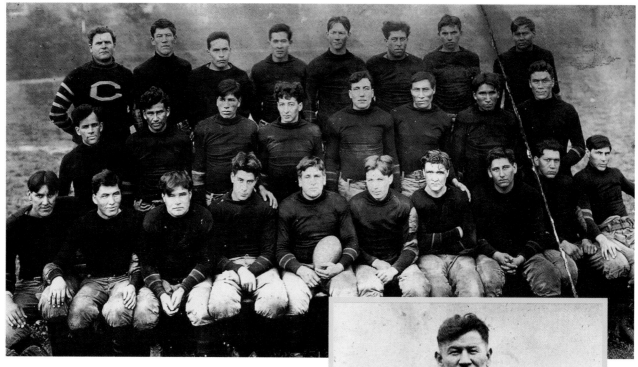

Thorpe's non-Olympic sports career included his college days with Carlisle (above), a stint with the Canton Bulldogs (right), one of professional football's first dominant teams, and five seasons as an outfielder for the New York Giants (opposite page, above), with whom he signed in 1913 (opposite page, below).

tis, who was himself part Native American, invited Thorpe to sit with him in the presidential box. When Thorpe did so, the entire crowd of 100,000 gave him a standing ovation. In 1951, the best athlete of the previous 50 years developed cancer of the lip and had to be hospitalized as a charity case. "We're broke," said his third wife, Patricia. "Jim has nothing but his name and his memories."

Thorpe died of a heart attack in 1953, still bereft of his medals. He was buried in Mauch Chunk, Pennsylvania, a town he had never set foot in but which agreed to change its name to Jim Thorpe in hopes of attracting tourists. In January of 1983, after a lengthy campaign by his daughter, Grace, Thorpe's Olympic medals were again presented to his family.

Aftermath

Americans have continued to dominate the Olympic decathlon, with 11 of the 20 gold medals awarded in the event going to U.S. athletes. As in the case of Thorpe, the decathlon has been a springboard to celebrity for the winners, as Bob Mathias (gold medalist in 1948 and 1952), Rafer Johnson (1960) and Bruce Jenner (1976) all went on to stake a notable place in the public consciousness. After a brief fall from prominence in the '80s, the United States returned to decathlon greatness in the '90s with world recordholder Dan O'Brien, arguably the greatest decathlete of all time, who took the gold at the '96 Games in Atlanta with an Olympic-record total of 8,824 points.

INDEX